CHI
energy of harmony

CHI
energy of harmony

solala towler

MQ Publications Ltd

Solala Towler is a musician, poet, and teacher. He is
editor of *The Empty Vessel, A Journal of Contemporary Taoism,*
a magazine with an international subscription and distribution
base (www.abodetao.com). He is author of *A Gathering
of Cranes: Bringing the Tao to the West* and *Embarking on the
Way: A Guide to Western Taoism,* and in the Tao Paths series,
Love, Harmony, Long Life, and *Good Fortune.* He is an instructor
of Taoist meditation and of several styles of chi kung. He has
taught classes and seminars all over the United States and
abroad and is president emeritus of the **National
Qigong Association** of the USA.

PUBLISHED BY MQ Publications Limited
12 The Ivories, 6–8 Northampton Street, London N1 2HY
Tel: 020 7359 2244   Fax: 020 7359 1616
email: mail@mqpublications.com

Copyright © MQ Publications Limited 2002

Text © Solala Towler 2002
DESIGN: **balley design**

ISBN: 1 84072 410 2

2 3 5 7 9 0 8 6 4

PRINTED AND BOUND IN CHINA

CONTENTS

INTRODUCTION

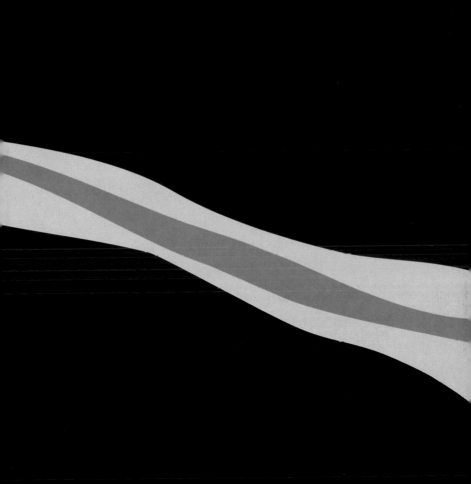

It can be said that the Chinese prize harmony above all things. Much, if not all, of classical Chinese literature is based on the idea of harmony.

Calligraphy, with its use of balance, harmony (and even the chi of the writer), from the preparation of food according to taste, element, and season, to the movement arts of tai chi and chi kung—all of these important parts of Chinese culture are based on the element of harmony.

It might be said that for the traditional Chinese, something that is disharmonious is worse than being ugly. Indeed, harmony is linked to beauty in a very real way. Harmony means that each element of a painting, a piece of calligraphy, a meal, or even a movement should be in balance with all other parts.

In a Chinese landscape painting, for example, all the elements are balanced with one another: the mountain rising up through the clouds, the lone pine tree jutting out bravely from its flanks, the small stream meandering quietly along at the bottom or the tiny figure sitting alone in his hut or crossing a bridge.

In traditional Chinese landscapes, the human figure is always the smallest, whereas in Western paintings, the opposite is usually true. In the Chinese tradition, humans are understood to be a small part of the natural world. If we are to remain in harmony with the world around us, we need to be reminded of this relationship.

By recognizing
and maintaining the
proper relationships between
the human and the natural
world, between the world outside
us and the world inside us, we
remain in harmony and balance.
This is the secret to long life,
happiness, good health, and
spiritual attainment.

For our chi, or integral life force, to remain strong, free-flowing, and well balanced, we need to know how to be in harmony with our surroundings but also with our own emotions, thoughts, feelings, and experiences.

By using the time-honored principles of the ancient Taoist classic, the *Tao Te Ching*, the energy practices of chi kung (developing the strength and power of the mind without straining the body), and the use of Taoist meditation or internal cultivation, we will explore the ideas and practices of harmony in our lives.

chapter one

HOW TO CREATE A HARMONIOUS LIFE *(TAO TE CHING)*

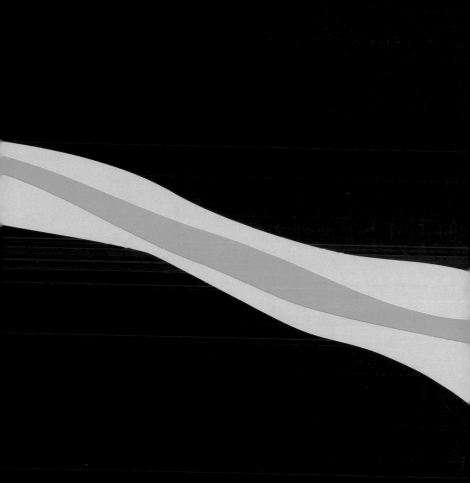

The Taoist classic book, the
Tao Te Ching, is said to have been
written some 2,500 years ago by
a sage called Lao-tzu, whose
name means "Old Boy."

Lao-tzu describes the sage as one who places
himself behind others in an attitude of humbleness,
and thus finds himself ahead. Because they are
selfless, they can succeed in all things.

The character for "sage," *tzu*, is also used as the character for "child." This term has been used to describe a sage or spiritual master.

A sage is somebody who is in total harmony with their world—the world around them as well as the world within them.

Lao-tzu tells us that the sage is guided by what he feels, rather than what he sees. Therefore he is nurtured not by the outside world but rather by what is inside.

Lao-tzu describes the ancient sages as "mysterious, subtle, and profound." Their depth of understanding was beyond our knowing because they were so profound we could never truly understand them, and can only describe them. They were carefree, like someone crossing a frozen river in winter. They were alert, like someone surrounded by danger on all sides. They were courteous, like a dignified guest.

The ancient sages moved in harmony with the world around them. They were also in touch with their own inner harmony and were able to base all their actions and movement on this state of awareness— what we might today call "a state of grace." They were yielding, like melting ice. They were sincere and unspoiled, like uncut jade. They were empty and open-minded, like a mountain gorge. And they were obscure, like muddy water.

Sages
or masters are so
called because they, in their
very being, embody the teachings
of the *Tao*. They have harmonized
all aspects of their being and are at one
with everything. But we do not have to
become sages to benefit from the
teachings of the *Tao Te Ching*. If we
take its words and images to heart,
we too can experience our own
being as "mysterious, subtle,
and profound."

How can we achieve the harmony
of the sage? One way is to use
the image of water. Lao-tzu tells us
that the highest virtue is to be like
water. Water, he says, benefits all
things, yet never contends.

Water always flows into the lowest level. It is colorless and it takes the shape of whatever container it finds itself in. It is patient yet very strong. Indeed, water, one of the softest substances in the world, can overcome the hardest substance. It carves canyons out of solid rock. If we take water as our guide, we learn to be soft, yielding, flexible, and humble, yet also patient and strong.

A potent symbol from the Chinese sages is the *yin/yang*. The yin/yang comprises the polarity of the universe, and the constant and enduring flux and transformation of all things.

The theory of yin/yang means that all of us have both a yin aspect as well as a yang aspect. This is natural and can be quite useful.

Yang has the qualities of aggression—an upward and outward direction. Yang is a light, fiery, and expansive energy.

Yin has the qualities of yielding in a downward and inward direction. Yin is dark, watery, and mysterious.

Yin could not exist without yang. Without the solid, earthly, foundation of yin, there would be nothing for the fiery, heavenly, expansionist energy, or yang, to push against.

Sometimes we identify with our yin aspect. We are in the mood to be nurtured, rather than nurturing; we feel soft and vulnerable; or we may retire to quieter, more inward experiences.

At some times we may identify with our yang aspect: We feel strong and adventurous, and we desire more exciting or creative experiences.

Oftentimes, the situation we find ourselves in requires either a yin or a yang response. To be able, at a moment's notice, to respond in an appropriate manner to whatever situation we find ourselves in is the mark of a sage.

An important Taoist concept is *wu wei*. Wu wei means not doing, or not doing anything that is against the natural flow. By becoming sensitive to the currents of energy in any given situation, we will be able to discern what the proper thing to do is. Sometimes the proper thing to do is to do nothing at all.

If we are in harmony with our outer environment, we have a better chance at being in harmony within. If we are not in harmony with ourselves, we often find ourselves out of harmony with our outside environment.

By following the words of Lao-tzu, we can find a path of inner harmony that will support us in times of conflict:

Yield and become whole.
Bend and you will become straight.
Empty yourself and you will become filled.
Though you grow old
You will be renewed.
Possess little and you will attain success.
Try to hold on to too much
And you will become confused.

Here we see that by trying to maintain control over our lives too tightly, we will lose ourselves. By trying to store up riches, we will become lost and confused.

33

how to create a **harmonious** life (*tao te ching*)

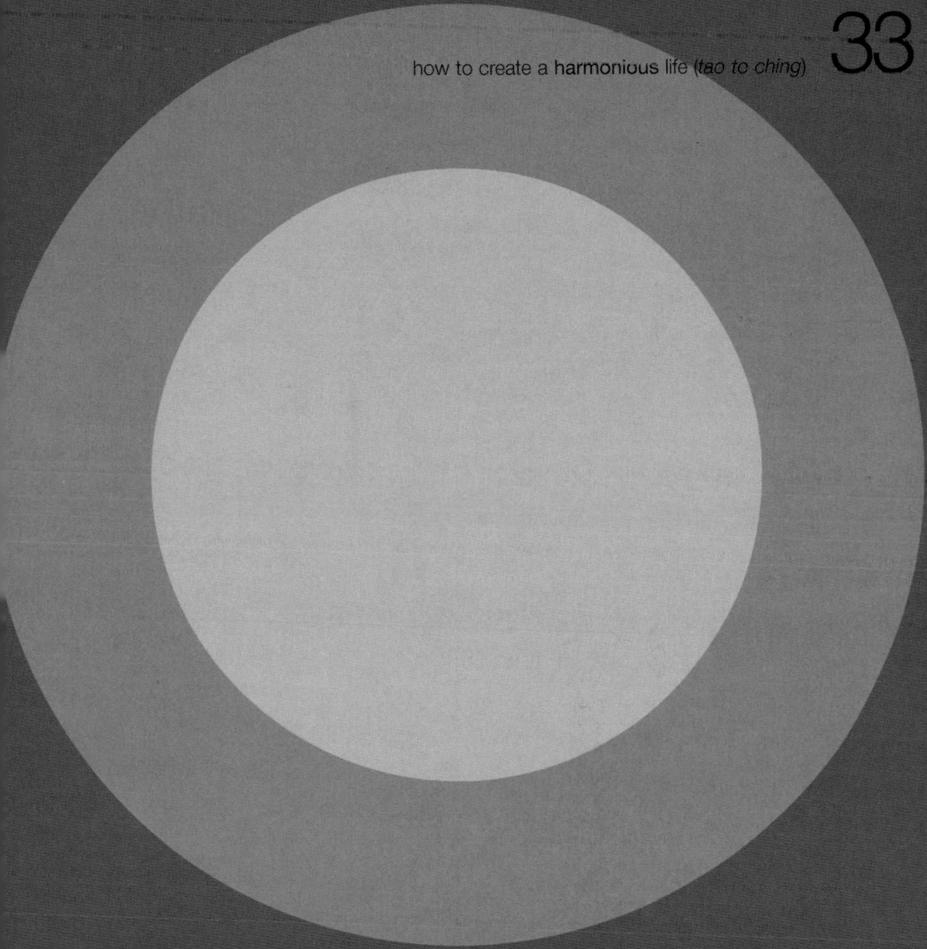

Many spiritual teachers have taught that maintaining inner harmony is more important than outer harmony. It is when we depend on outside circumstances for our inner harmony that we often find ourselves in trouble.

If we do not seek for ourselves, if we are willing to yield, to surrender ourselves, we will not only be successful but will live long and happy lives.

Lao-tzu also says:

Overfill a bowl
And it will run over.
Sharpen a blade too much
And it will lose its edge.
Pile up riches
And you will not be able to protect them.
Just complete the tasks before you,
Then withdraw when your work is done.
This is the way of heaven.

To overdo something, even when it is a good thing, will lead to ruin. But if we carefully deal with what is right in front of us, we can then rest in the knowledge that we are acting in a natural and harmonious fashion.

By remaining in harmony with our own wants, desires, dreams, and ideas of how things "should be," we can find a way to deal harmoniously with the way things "really are."

By becoming a person with inner harmony and peace, we will bring that sense of harmony and peace to everyone we come into contact with.

chapter two

THE WAY
OF INNER
HARMONY (MEDITATION)

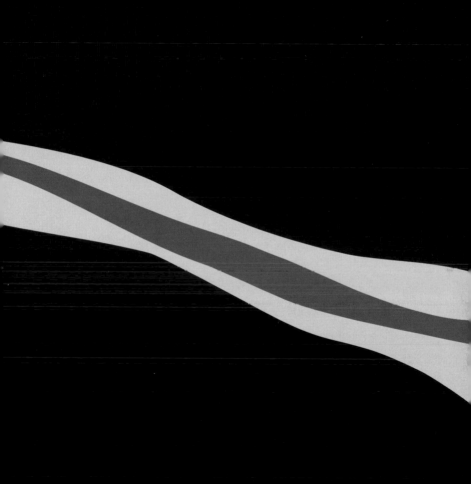

When most
people hear the term
"meditation," they think of an
austere practice that involves
sitting in an uncomfortable
position for an interminable time,
trying hard not to think of anything
while the mind races madly and
the legs and back cramp up.
Or they think of sitting high in
the mountains, leaving their
earthly forms behind, and
soaring into the realm
of infinity.

Others may come up with a picture of rows and rows of silent bodies sitting long into the night, trying to transcend "normal" consciousness and attain some sort of enlightened state that will immediately solve all their earthly problems.

Meditation can contain aspects of the practices that immediately pop into your head when you hear it mentioned, but at its core it is much more simple, direct, and easier to learn and make a part of your everyday life.

However, for many people, the practice of meditation can be the most difficult, painful, and challenging experience of their lives. It can raise issues that have been buried so deep that they have been successfully ignored for a lifetime. It can bring one to the very brink of one's sanity, or it can bore one to tears.

Meditation, practiced correctly and regularly in the way that is most appropriate for each individual, can open doorways into worlds that we can only imagine. It can open lines of communication to the world of helping and healing spirits, and can bring one closer to one's idea of God, *Tao*, the Eternal, or the Great Mystery.

Taoist meditation is not just a relaxation practice, though it does have that function. It is not simply a quest for a higher state of consciousness, but seeks to balance mind, body, and spirit into one unified field. It utilizes mind, body, and spirit as well as the life force or energy that animates all living things (including humans, animals, plants, and even planets), which the Taoists call *chi*.

There are many reasons to begin a meditation practice—from cutting down on stress in your life to maintaining energy levels to improve longevity. The more you can erase the line between when you are doing your meditation or spiritual practices and when you are living the rest of your life, the better.

Human beings have always meditated. The oldest cultures, including those from India as well as China, have used various meditation practices to maintain health, stamina, and vitality, as well as to commune with the source of all life. All of these reasons are valid to begin or maintain a meditation practice.

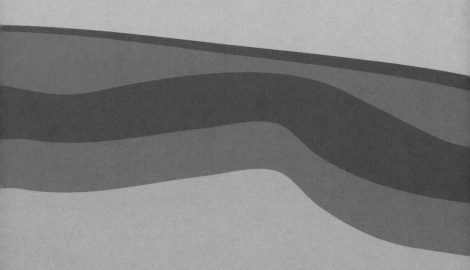

Meditation has long been used as a tool for achieving inner harmony. Meditation can be done in various ways: moving, standing, sitting, or even lying down. The goal of meditation is to achieve a level or experience of peacefulness, relaxation, and an opening to one's deeper or hidden nature.

Lao-tzu says:

> Strive to become empty,
> Maintain tranquillity and peace.
> As the ten thousand things
> Come into being,
> Silently observe their return
> To nonbeing.

By creating an atmosphere of detachment from the comings and goings of the world, the "ten thousand things," we will not get so caught up in these distractions and instead, find a place of peace and tranquillity.

By slowing down, by paying attention to our breath, and allowing our minds to move slowly and deeply, we can reach new levels of understanding about ourselves, as well as the world around us.

EXERCISE

Sit on a cushion, or on the edge of a chair if you prefer. Either close your eyes or keep them open lightly. Breathe slowly and deeply through your nose and from your belly, using your diaphragm to really fill and empty your lungs from the bottom up.

Now concentrate your internal vision on the space below your navel in the lower abdomen. This space is called the lower *dan tien*, or "field of elixir." By concentrating on this space you will be able to build a strong foundation of chi, or internal energy.

Begin by counting your breaths on each inhale and each exhale. Count up to ten, and then begin again. This will help your mind to have something to concentrate on, cutting down on some of the cluttered thoughts about the day's business that often pop up when we begin to meditate.

As you inhale, breathe in clear or golden light or healing chi. Feel it enter every cell of your body, filling it with light.

As you exhale, let go of all tensions, toxins, pain, or any negative energy you feel in your body. Imagine it flowing out of you like dark smoke.

EXERCISE

Another way to meditate, called "sitting in tranquillity," is to just sit and breathe. Thinking of nothing, envisioning nothing, we merely sit and let ourselves "be breathed." In this we simply allow ourselves time to be. This can have a wonderfully rejuvenating effect on both your body and spirit.

Lao-tzu describes
this type of meditation as
"sitting and letting the mind settle."
Often our minds and emotions can
be likened to a muddy pond of water.
In this state we are unclear and turbulent
and our light is dim. But if we sit and let
the mud settle to the bottom of the
pond, we can be like clear water
with sunlight shining through
from above.

EXERCISE

Stand with your arms out in front of you in a half-circle, as if you are hugging someone. With your mind intent, send roots twice your height down into the earth. Feel yourself stabilize and become rooted into it. Stand there for five to twenty minutes, drawing healing yin energy up from the earth.

EXERCISE

You can meditate lying down. The famous Taoist master Chen Tuan practiced sleeping meditation for months at a time.

Lie on your back. Palms may be facing up or down. Concentrate, as before, on breathing slowly and deeply into your lower *dan tien*. Feel your abdomen expand during the inhale and contract during the exhale. Continue to lie there, breathing in and out, and imagine that you are receiving healing chi from the universe. At the very least it will be a nice relaxing practice!

Sometimes in Taoist meditation, we work on gently guiding our chi throughout our meridians or special pathways, such as the *du mo*, which runs up the back of the body along the spine, and the *ren mo*, which runs down the front of the body.

If you have a place of pain, breathe the chi energy into that area by guiding it with your mind, in a gentle and nonforceful manner. Feel it fill that area with light and healing.

If we wish to live in harmony with the world, we need to be able to live in harmony with ourselves. By learning how to sit or stand or lie in meditation, we can become more harmonious and peaceful beings.

When we meditate, we are "doing nothing" in the best Taoist tradition!

Because we in the West are so caught up in "doing," it can seem frivolous or even shameful to be "not doing." But by "not doing," we can reach areas of ourselves that all the "doing" in the world could never begin to reach.

Even when we do nothing,
we can still work on our
breathing, our sense of serenity,
our sense of acceptance,
our sense of openness, and
our sense of surrender.

Even when we are sick or laid up from an injury, we can use that time to meditate successfully.

By this kind of "doing nothing," we can do some of the very important inner work that we are often too busy to attend to—or would rather not face—when we are well.

By using our "down" time to do this kind of inner work, we often find that when we are able to get back to our daily lives they will be all the more enriched for it.

Taoists have always studied nature. They watched how animals rested, how they curled up to lie down, or, like the stork, stood on one leg. They incorporated all these observations into their meditation and movement practices (there is more on this in Chapter 4).

Meditation is the perfect way to harmonize your inner being with your outer being. By allowing your mind to focus on your breath, you can balance both sides of your brain, or your *yin* and *yang* natures.

By allowing ourselves to "be breathed," we can find that still center in the very midst of our noisy, clamoring minds, which will lead us to the understanding and awareness of our higher or deeper self.

Once we have glimpsed and then experienced this deep inner nature, we will begin to move it, in a deeply harmonious manner, into our lives.

The act of meditation helps us to harmonize ourselves in a way that is non-forceful, gentle, and long-lasting.

Meditation then becomes not something you do for a limited time period to achieve a certain goal, but instead something that you do as a part of living, like breathing itself.

chapter three

THE WAY
OF INNER
BALANCE

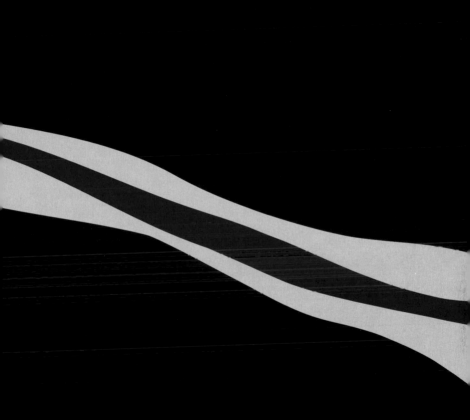

In order for true harmony to exist we must learn how to live in a state with both inner and outer balance.

Outer balance can be maintained by proper diet, exercise, a good environment, and the practice of *tai chi* or *chi kung*.

Internal balance is perhaps more difficult to attain and maintain. It can be a combination of emotions, attitudes, mindset, and feelings about your life and the world we live in.

For the Chinese, the perfect sense of balance is embodied in the idea of *yin/yang*. Often mistakenly referred to as yin *and* yang, yin/yang is simply two sides of a unified whole.

The classic symbol for yin/yang looks like two fish swimming in a circle around each other. The tail of one is formed from the head of the other.

In this way we see that yin/yang are born out of each other and are transformed into each other.

Each of yin/yang contains the seed of the other. There is a tiny seed circle of dark yin contained in the white part of yang, as there is a seed circle of white yang contained in the darkness of yin.

Originally, yin stood for the shady side of a hill, and yang stood for the sunny side. Eventually, they came to be used as a symbol of the polarity of the universe.

A "yin" activity is one that leads us inward, such as meditation, contemplation, walking, reading, or listening to music.

"Yang" activities are of a more outward nature. They include sports, martial arts, running, or playing a musical instrument.

By participating in both types of activity, we are able to balance ourselves, both internally and externally, thereby achieving harmony in our lives.

Yin energy must have the fiery, moving quality of yang to stir it up and prevent it from becoming stagnant.

It is important to remember that yin/yang is always
moving. Just as the symbol of the two fish swirl
around and around, created out of each
other and transforming into each other,
the universe itself is in a constant
state of flux and motion.

We also live in our own
world of yin/yang. Our own
light and dark sides are
constantly changing and
rebalancing themselves.

Sometimes our energy is up, at other times it is down. Sometimes we feel ourselves drawn into an outward, dynamic, even aggressive manner. At other times we seek rest, retreat, and quiet. This is all part of the interplay of yin/yang.

Knowing when we need to act in a yang or more aggressive manner, and when we need to act in a yin or more inwardly directed manner is the way to inner balance and harmony.

We all have a yin nature as well as a yang nature, and we all need to be able to experience these two different yet supporting facets of ourselves.

An interesting exercise is to work on expressing the side of ourselves that we don't usually reveal. By allowing the opposite side of our nature to emerge, we can often discover new aspects of ourselves. If your yin nature is the more dominant, try to be more assertive within your life and your relationships than you would usually be, getting in touch with your more fiery yang nature. If your yang nature is the more dominant, try slowing down, listening more, and being more willing to try someone else's ideas instead of your own.

An important
aspect of yin/yang is
their ability to transform
into each other. What this
often means is that any
situation, good or bad,
when taken to an extreme,
will transform into
its opposite.

Often, our
greatest lessons and
what we might regard as
our greatest gifts may come
at our times of greatest adversity.
Likewise, when we are riding high
and perhaps not looking out for
ourselves as we should, we
can also come to our
greatest fall.

Remember that
inside each dark moment
is the seed of future light, and
within each bright moment is
the seed of future unrest. If we
can pay attention to these
things, we can often forestall
or avoid problems
altogether.

Besides yin/yang, there is also the concept of *wu hsing*, or the Five Elements. We are all made up of a combination of each of these five elements and their correspondences. Each of the five elements also corresponds to both a positive and a negative emotion.

The first of the five elements is wood. This corresponds to spring, the color green, the direction east or the sunrise, the liver organ, and the energy of new beginnings. Wood corresponds to the negative emotion of anger and the positive quality of flexibility and free-flowingness.

The second of the five elements is fire. Fire corresponds to summer, the color red, the direction south, the heart, and the energy of joy and creativity. Fire corresponds to the negative emotion of hysteria.

The third element is earth, the time between each season, the color yellow, the direction of center, the spleen and the energy of groundedness and connection to all life. Earth corresponds to the negative emotion of self-absorption or worry and the positive quality of empathy and groundedness.

The fourth of the five elements is metal or gold, which corresponds to fall, the color white, the direction west, the lungs, and the energy of contraction or "bringing in the harvest." Metal corresponds to the negative emotion of grief and the positive quality of courage.

The fifth of the five elements is water and corresponds to winter, the direction north, the color black or blue-black, the kidneys, and the energy of "returning to the source." Water corresponds to the negative emotion of fear and the positive quality of will and determination.

By being aware of
each of the qualities of
the five elements within
ourselves, and our ability to
connect and support the
positive qualities we each
possess, we can both
balance and harmonize
our inner being.

When we can meditate on our ability to feel our sense of flexibility or free-flowingness, our joy and creativity, our sense of groundedness and connection to the earth, our ability to accept life's challenges with courage and determination, then we will see ourselves as the bright and shining beings we truly are.

By seeking out our places of anger, hysteria, self-absorption, grief, and fear, we can also begin to heal ourselves, one step at a time, one moment at a time.

To reach true harmony is to become balanced, with our yin/yang nature comfortable and constantly evolving, and each of the five elements of our being interconnected with each other.

As we continue to see ourselves
as the sum of all of our parts, as
a constantly shifting experience of
yin/yang and the five elements,
we can begin to come into
perfect and effortless harmony,
both with our internal world and
the world around us.

chapter four

HARMONY AND
INTERNAL
STRENGTH (*CHI KUNG*)

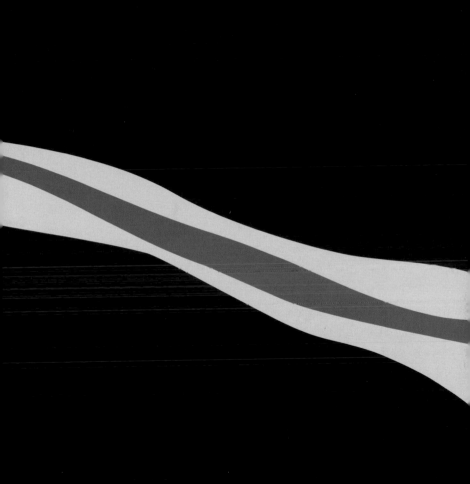

The term *chi kung* (pronounced "chee gong") is made up of two characters. The first one, "chi," means the basic life force of the universe. It is what animates us, what warms us, keeps our organs in their places and directs all our movements.

The character "kung" means work, or something that takes effort and time. Thus, the term "chi kung" means working with energy; work that will take effort and time to become fruitful.

There are different types of *chi kung*, some quite vigorous and some sublimely simple. Effects will vary, according to the skill level of the practitioner, the consistency of the practice, and his or her age and relative health. No matter what style you choose, all chi kung deals with accessing, circulating, and storing chi, or vital force, within the body.

100 chi energy of harmony

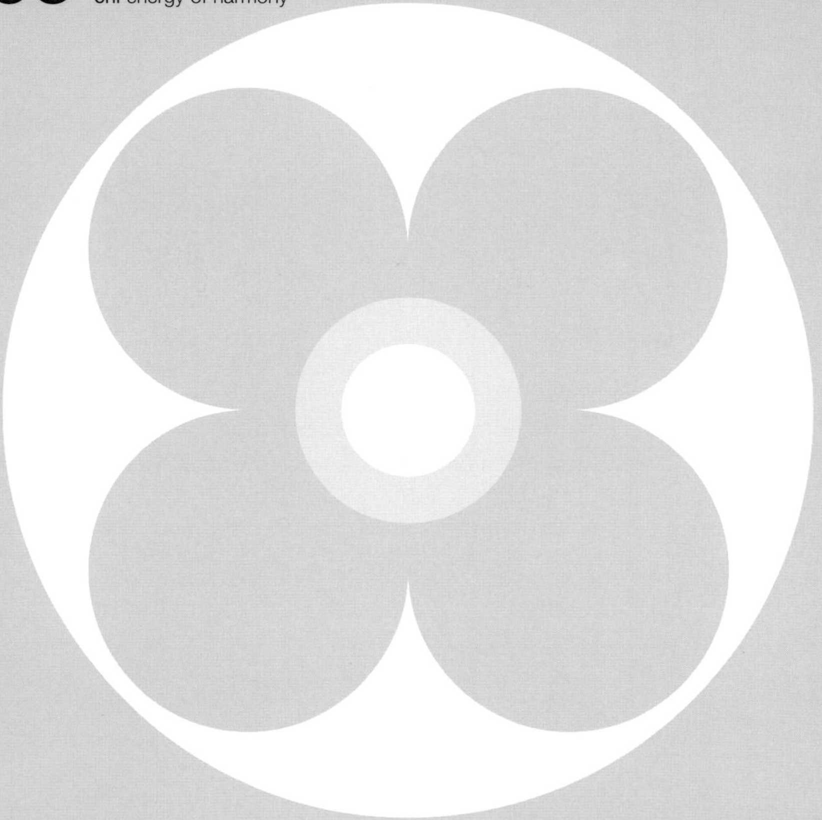

Many people in the West are familiar with the slow-moving dancelike movements called tai chi, translated as "great ultimate fist." Not as many people realize that it is a form of *chi kung*. Like other forms of *chi kung*, it works with the principles of rootedness, balance, and a smooth flow of energy throughout the body. It is at once a playful dance of yin and yang and a powerful form of self-defense.

Tai chi is not just about moving your body in elegant circles. It is about being able to tap into the very flow of the universe, the dance of energy as it moves through your being and as it is expressed by you personally.

Find a teacher who can pass on the principles and the postures in such a way that you can make them your own, through practice, through perseverance, through discovery of your own nature. Then you can find your own expression of the *Tao* through tai chi.

In tai chi practice, we learn how to push forward and how to yield, how to balance, first on one foot then the other, and how to sink our energy deep within our bellies (our *dan tien*—see Chapter 2). We also learn how to maintain our composure and our inner stillness, even while moving. This is why tai chi is often called "stillness within movement."

By learning how
to keep a calm and
balanced center while
moving backward and
forward, from side to side,
and sometimes in a complete
circle, we can learn how to
maintain a sense of balance
and centeredness in the
rest of our lives.

Principles that we learn in tai chi practice help us to lead more harmonious and effective lives in our business relationships, as well as in our personal relationships. An argument in which both sides are feeling aggressive and defensive can often escalate until one or both say or do things they later regret. By using the tai chi principles of when to be aggressive and when to retreat, or when to deflect negative energy with emptiness, the confrontation can often be easily defused.

The art of *chi kung* requires hard work and perseverance. Significant changes cannot be brought about in a single weekend workshop. It takes time to reroute the often unnatural flows of chi that have built up in our bodies. It can take years of practice to heal long-lasting health problems or to build up enough vital chi so that new health problems do not occur. It can take a lifetime of practice to be able to align one's chi with the chi of the universe and be able to transcend the physical world as we know it, at the point of death or before. But all along the way there are rewards and benefits for anyone who pursues a regular practice.

The positive results can be of a physical, emotional, psychological, or spiritual nature, or a combination of all four. Practicing *chi kung* will make you healthier, more emotionally centered, psychologically balanced, smarter, attractive, creative, and happier; it will strengthen your will and develop your character, and more!

All *chi kung* practice concerns the accessing, circulating, and storing of chi as well as the directing, toning, and building of a strong current of chi in the body. The various chi pathways in the body include meridians such as the *du mai* (which flows up the back), the *ren mai* (which flows down the front), the *belt channel* (which flows around the waist), the *chong mai* (which flows directly through the center of the body), the major yin channels (which flow along the inside of the arms and legs), and the major yang channels (which flow along the outside of the arms and legs).

Chi kung also works with the chi field that is located both inside and outside the body. Passing the hands down the front or the back of the body can affect one's internal organs, because of the relationship between the outer and inner chi field. This is also how high-level martial artists can injure or even kill someone with one blow.

Chi kung practice, which combines deep and regular breathing, slow movements, and correct visualization, can have a profound effect on our entire systems.

Regular practice of *chi kung* will make you healthier, more emotionally balanced, smarter, sexier, and more stabilized and harmonious in your personal as well as professional life.

Western medicine, although it can be highly effective in certain acute situations, often has little to offer to people with long-term, chronic problems, such as fibro-myalgia, chronic fatigue syndrome, and MS.

But with dedicated
chi kung practice, many of
these chronic problems can be
dealt with much more effectively.
The gains may be slow in coming
but with perseverance, you will find
that your stamina becomes
stronger and your symptoms
will very often diminish.

It is like putting money into a bank. You may only be putting a few dollars in every day but, little by little, it builds up and before you know it you have a large reserve to draw upon.

Chi is very subtle—and can even seem magical—but it is very real and can be felt in many ways, from the sensation of an electrical current that the *chi kung* master gives to his or her patients to the feeling of being whole and happy and alive in your body.

The following are some ways that you can begin to feel the flow of chi in your own body. Go slowly and pay attention. At first the feelings may be very subtle, but with time they will become stronger.

EXERCISE

An easy way to feel chi is to create a chi ball between your two palms. Hold them out in front of you at shoulder or waist height, facing each other. Now imagine there is a solid ball of energy between them, about the size of a beach ball. Then gently push your hands together, squeezing the ball between them. Next, expand the ball by pulling your hands apart. Do this simple exercise a few times and you will begin to feel a subtle yet solid, rubbery presence between your palms.

Chi kung is not merely a health exercise, but an approach to life itself. It is a state of mind characterized by complete relaxation, and complete acceptance, deep meditation and love, joy, and beneficence, renewal and rebirth; it is open to the healing energy of the universe, and it offers healing for the whole world.

EXERCISE

A simple yet effective exercise is to stand quietly for a few moments, then bring your arms slowly up in front of you, palms facing down, to shoulder level. Then slowly lower them to waist level. This raises your central chi to the heart center, then back down to the lower *dan tien*. It is an effective way to balance and center your energy. Try it at least nine times and see if you feel a difference in your sense of balance and well-being.

Chi kung is a way to access the energy of the universe and make it our own. It is a way to help our own internal energy flow smoothly and strongly throughout our bodies. It is a way to open our spiritual eyes, to be able to see beyond what our physical eyes can reach. It is an attentive attitude of openness and grace, an exchange on a deep and basic level of one's inner being and that of the great undivided, unending, undissolved *Tao*.

With the exchange of energy comes balance, harmony, composure of spirit, deepening of character, and the relaxing of the mind muscles. It brings a feeling of safety, of being at home, of being empty and full at the same time. It helps you to be clear of vision, open-hearted, soft yet strong, and sensitive to changes in the energetic atmosphere. It gives you compassion for the sufferings of those around you, a sense of proportion and objectivity, and an openness to change, transformation, and miracles.

How do we make sure that our chi is harmonized and flowing strongly? Initially, by paying attention to the ebbs and flows of our internal energy as we go through our day. Notice how the chi feels or changes according to your activities.

When our chi is calm, we are calm. When it is disrupted or flowing erratically, we will feel like a storm is blowing within us.

We can often correct such imbalances by using the simple chi exercises mentioned earlier. Meditation, herbs, diet, acupuncture, massage, rest, and relaxation are all important parts of a healthy chi life.

Remembering to breathe properly is also an important aspect of chi cultivation. Really feel those in-breaths coming from deep in your lower *dan tien* and filling your lungs from the bottom up.

When you exhale, really feel the breath as well as any tensions, toxins, pain, or disease leaving your body like a fine mist. Offer it up to the universe, God, or the earth itself, to be transformed into light.

An important aspect of chi cultivation is to go slowly. In whatever activity, or even in our communications with others, it is always best not to be in a hurry. When we hurry, we are more likely to be off-balance and make mistakes or cause accidents.

By going slowly we can be better attuned to each present moment and be better able to make sure that all of our actions and decisions come from our authentic self.

Practices such as tai chi, *chi kung*, yoga, or even walking can give us a sense of what it feels like to move slowly and gracefully through our lives.

Chi is all around us all the time. The very air we breathe, the food we eat, the water we drink, the feeling we get when we look at the stars at night and the sun in the daytime, our interactions with our friends, family, and community—all these things are filled with chi.

Paying attention to each detail of our activity can also be an interesting way of meditation. Being carefully attuned to each aspect of our activity, paying close attention to each step, each movement, each way we turn, can give us insight into whether we are going through our activities in a balanced and harmonious manner.

EXERCISE

Here is a simple chi exercise that can be done whenever you feel ungrounded, uncentered, disturbed, or confused.

Simply stand with your feet shoulder-width apart, arms down at the sides. Bend slowly at the knees and use your palms to scoop healing yin energy up from the earth.

Slowly bring the arms, palms up, to the level of your upper *dan tien* or third eye. Then turn your palms over and gently guide the energy down the front of your body, awakening all of your organs and spiritual centers there.

When your hands reach the level of your navel, move your arms out to the sides, making a big circle, and bring your palms together, right over left, and place them over your lower *dan tien* or lower abdomen.

Do this exercise about nine times, or even more if you like. Imagine your chi field getting bigger with each circle, until it is as large as the world around you.

Stand for a few moments with your palms over your lower *dan tien* and breathe deeply and slowly, feeling that great field of chi you are now standing within. To end, circle your palms over your navel nine times in one direction and then nine times in the other direction. Open your eyes, take one more deep breath, and re-enter the world.

By not indulging in activities that we know rob us of our chi, by not allowing our eyes to gaze on unpleasant or disturbing images, by not indulging ourselves in morbid or depressing thought patterns, we can allow our chi to remain strong and clear.

By remaining as calm as we can in any given moment, by not allowing our emotions or thought processes to carry our energy away, we can remain centered and strong and our chi will also remain centered and strong within us.